Ethnology Of Egyptian Sudan

Keane, A. H. (Augustus Henry), 1833-1912

ETHNOLOGY OF EGYPTIAN SUDÁN.

BY

PROF. A. H. KEANE, B.A.,

MEMBER OF COUNCIL ANTHROPOLOGICAL INSTITUTE; CORRESPONDING MEMBER ITALIAN AND
WASHINGTON ANTHROPOLOGICAL SOCIETIES

[Reprinted from the Journal of the Anthropological Institute, November, 1884.]

LONDON:
EDWARD STANFORD, CHARING CROSS.

1884.

Price Two Shillings.

ETHNOLOGY *of* EGYPTIAN SUDÁN.

By Prof. A. H KEANE, B A

THE decline of Christian and expansion of Muhammadan influences in many parts of North Africa in recent times are curiously illustrated by the fate of the terms *Nigritia, Negroland,* which in modern geographical nomenclature have been superseded by the synonymous Arabic word *Sudán,* or, more fully, *Beled-es-Sudán,* "Land of the Blacks" This expression is properly applied to the whole region lying between the Atlantic and Red Sea, and stretching from the Sahara and Egypt towards the Equator It comprises three physically distinct divisions, West, Central, and East Sudán, draining respectively through the Niger, Senegambia, and some smaller coast streams to the Atlantic, through the Shary and Komadugu to the Tsad depression, through the Nile to the Mediterranean. Ethnically it is regarded by Lepsius[1] as a land of transition between the Hamites of North, and the Negroes of South Africa, the only indigenous elements recognised by him in the Dark Continent. As G. A Krause,[2] then most recent observer, is inclined to group the Fulahs with the Hamites, this view may be accepted as fairly representing the actual conditions in West and Central Sudán

But in East Sudán, which here alone concerns us, the relations are far more complex. Since its incorporation in the possessions of the Khedive, this region is commonly known as Egyptian Sudán, and although official documents recognise the presence of two peoples only, the Arabs and Negroes,[3] it is really the converging point of nearly all the African races. The salient geographical feature of the land is its great artery, the Nile, along whose main sections are roughly distributed the chief divisions of the inhabitants. Thus in the extreme south the Somerset Nile, connecting Lakes Victoria and Albert Nyanza, flows nearly altogether through BANTU territory The Bahr-el-Jebel, that is, the section between Lake Albert and the Sobat confluence, is essentially NEGRO domain The White Nile proper, that is, the section between the Sobat and Blue Nile confluences, as well as the main stream thence northwards to Dongola, is occupied on its left bank almost exclusively by SEMITES, on its right partly by Semites, partly by HAMITES. From Dongola to Asuan on the Egyptian frontier, the narrow valley hemmed in between the escarpments of the Libyan and Arabian Deserts, is held, with one or two slight interruptions, by NUBIANS. Then the whole region east of this valley, as far

as the Red Sea, and from Abyssinia to Egypt, belongs to the
Hamites, whose territory, with one interruption above Massawah,
also stretches between the Abyssinian highlands and the coast
round to Cape Gardafui, and thence southwards to the Equator
The arid wastes and steppes west of the Nile are held entirely
by Semite nomads, while in the outlying provinces of Kordofan
and Dar-Fur, Semites, Nubians, Negroes, and, in the extreme
west, even Hamites and Fulahs, are diversely intermingled.
Grouped along the course of the great artery we thus find
Bantus and Negroes in the south, Semites and Hamites in the
centre, Nubians in the north.

I. The Bantus.

The Bantus are represented mainly by the Wa-ganda and
Wa-nyoro of the native states of U-ganda and U-nyoro, lying
north and west of Lake Victoria. Although officially included
in the Egyptian province of the "Equator" (Hat-el-Istwa), they
have never been reduced, hence lie rather beyond the scope of
the present inquiry Here it will suffice to remark that they
occupy the widest range of any people in Africa, being in
almost exclusive possession of the southern half of the continent
At some points they even encroach four or five degrees of
latitude north of the Equator, while their territory is limited in
the extreme south and south-west by a considerable enclave
occupied by the Hottentots and Bushmen. At the same time
the Bantus themselves have no ethnical coherency, and it seems
impossible to recognise a distinct Bantu type in an anthropological sense. They are essentially Negroid rather than Negro
peoples, presenting every shade of transition, from the pure
Negro of Guinea and the Sudán, to the pure Hamite and
Semite of the Middle Nile and north-east coast Between
these two extremes they oscillate in endless variety, offering
nowhere any stable physical features, and bound together only
by their common Bantu speech. Hence, as I have elsewhere
remarked,[4] the expression Bantu, intelligible in a linguistic
sense, has no definite ethnological meaning. But for the fact
that most of the peoples occupying the southern half of the
continent speak dialects of a common mother-tongue, no
anthropologist would ever have thought of grouping them
together, as forming a separate division of mankind. Bantu
thus corresponds to the analogous terms Aryan, Finno-Tatar,
Malayo-Polynesian, Athabascan, in other regions of the globe,
terms which have their proper place rather in philological than
in anthropological writings.

II THE NEGROES.

Numerically the Negro is by far the most important element in Egyptian Sudán   It is in almost undisturbed possession, not only of the main stream from the great lakes to and beyond the Sobat junction, but also of the Sobat valley itself, and of the countless headwaters of the White Nile converging from the west and south-west at Lake No above the Sobat junction. Within this area is probably concentrated one-half of the population of the whole Nile basin, from the equatorial lakes to the Mediterranean, a population which has been roughly estimated at about forty millions   Here are several large and powerful Negro nations, some still enjoying political autonomy, such as the Zandeh (Nyam-Nyam), the Mittu, and the Monbuttu, who occupy the low water-parting between the Nile, Congo, and Tsad basins, some brought within the limits of the Khedive's possessions, such as the Bari and Nuer of the Bahr-el-Jebel, the Bongo (Doi), Rol, and Krej of the western affluents of the White Nile, the Funj of Senaar, and the Shilluks and Dinkas about the Sobat confluence. The most numerous and wide-spread are the Zandeh, the eastern portion of whose territory has alone been explored. They are divided into several inde-pendent states, stretching from the Bahr-el-Jebel half across the continent, probably to the territory of the Fans in the far West

Of the reduced nations, the Shilluks and Dinkas are by far the most important   The Shilluks appear to be of the same stock as the Funj of Senaar, who by fusion with the Arabs formed a powerful kingdom, which in the last century extended northwards beyond the Atbara confluence. Of the Dinkas, who number several millions, as many as twenty-five distinct tribes are mentioned by D G Beltrame,[5] who has resided several years amongst the native communities of the White Nile

Although grouped as Negroes proper, very few of these Nilotic peoples present the ideal type of the Blacks, such as we find it amongst the Ashantís and other inhabitants of Upper Guinea. The complexion is in general less black, the nose less flat, the lips less protruding, the hair less woolly, the dolicho-cephaly and prognathism less marked—in a word, the salient features of the Negro race less prominent than elsewhere. Apart from the more minute shades of transition due to diverse intermingling with the Hamites and Semites,[6] two distinct types may be plainly distinguished—one black and long-headed (Shilluk, Dinka, Nuer, Mittu), the other reddish or ruddy brown and short-headed (Bongo, Zandeh, &c) The complexion of the latter may possibly be due to the properties of the red earth prevalent in their districts.[7] But no theory has been advanced to account for their brachycephaly, which is all the more difficult to explain, inasmuch as it is characteristic neither of the aboriginal Negro, nor of the intruding Hamite and Semite elements.

Schweinfurth tells us that the Bongos are "hardly removed from the lowest grade of brachycephaly" (*op. cit*, i, 263), and the same is largely true of the Zandeh But this feature appears to be altogether far more general amongst the Negro races than is usually supposed. Of the eighteen skulls from Equatorial Africa in the Barnard Davis collection (now in the museum of the College of Surgeons, London), as many as four are distinctly round-headed Craniology thus fails in Negroland as it does in so many other regions, as a constant factor in determining racial types.

The Nilotic races appear to form a connecting link between those of Baghirmi in the Tsad basin, and the non-Bantu peoples between the Kilima-Njaro highlands and the east side of the Victoria Nyanza, who have been recently visited by the Rev. T Wakefield and Mr Thomson. The Wa-Kavirondo nation of this region are allied in speech to the Shilluks and the Yambu of the Sobat valley.[8] The language of their neighbours, the Oigob (Masai), also presents a remarkable peculiarity in the presence of grammatical gender, which it has in common with all the dialects of the Nilotic Negroes, except the Dinka[9] This point is of great philological interest, grammatical gender being a feature hitherto supposed to be restricted to the three inflecting families (Aryan, Semitic, and Hamitic), besides the Hottentot by Lepsius partly on this ground affiliated to the Hamitic. In Oigob gender, represented by *l* masculine, and *n* feminine, is fully developed Thus: *ol* = he, that man, *il* = those men; *en, eng* = she, *ing* = those women, *el-e* = this man; *en-a* = this woman, with which compare the Bari: *lo* = this man; *na* = this woman; the Bongo: *bah* = he, *hoh* = she, and the Shilluk: *nenno* = he, *náno* = she. Lepsius, however, is inclined to regard the so-called gender particles of the Oigob simply as "class prefixes" analogous to those of the Bantu system They certainly seem to indicate, besides sex, the qualities of strength, vigour, courage (masculine), or else anything soft, effeminate, weak or delicate (feminine). Thus the Masai call themselves *il Oigob* = "the men," using the masculine particle, whereas their Wa-Kwafi neighbours are stigmatised with the feminine particle, as *im-Barawino*, plural *em-Barawin*, implying weakness or effeminacy. It is also noteworthy that, as with the Bantu prefixes, the masculine and feminine articles are repeated in a more or less modified form, both before the noun and its adjective. Thus. *ol-doeno o-ibor* = the-mountain the-white (masculine); *en-anga na-ibor* = the-dress the-white (feminine) These forms are most instructive as probably supplying the crude beginning of the highly developed alliterative Bantu system on the one hand, and on the other those of true grammatical gender as fully elaborated in the higher orders of inflecting speech. Compare, for instance, with the foregoing examples, the Zulu-Kafir. *in-Kose en-Kulu* = the-chief the-great; and the Latin· *domin-a me-a* = lady-the my-the, where the parallelism between the respective initial and final "euphonic concords" is obvious Here also we see how the different morphological orders of speech merge imperceptibly one in the other, and how groundless is the new philological doctrine that these several orders are definitely fixed, and, like Cuvier's animal and vegetable species, incapable of further transformation.

Although Islám has made considerable progress, especially amongst the Funj of Senaar, the Shilluks, Dinkas, and other Nilotic Negro tribes, the bulk of the people are still practically nature-worshippers Witchcraft continues to flourish amongst the Equatorial tribes, and important events are almost everywhere attended by sanguinary rites When preparing for battle the "medicine-man" flays an infant and places the bleeding victim on the war-path to be trampled by the warriors marching to victory. Cannibalism also, in some of its most repulsive forms, prevails amongst the Nyam-Nyam, who barter in human fat as a universal staple of trade, and amongst the Monbuttu who cure for future use the bodies of the slain in battle, and "drive their prisoners before them, as butchers drive sheep to the shambles, and these are only reserved to fall victims on a later day to their horrible and sickly greediness"[10] Yet many of these peoples are skilled agriculturists, and cultivate some of the useful industries, such as iron smelting and casting, weaving and pottery, with great success. The form and ornamental designs of their utensils display real artistic taste, while the temper of their iron implements is often superior to that of the imported European hardware Here again the observation has been made, that the tribes most addicted to cannibalism also excel in mental qualities and physical energy. Nor are they strangers to the finer feelings of human nature, and above all the surrounding peoples the Zandeh anthropophagists are distinguished by their regard and devotion for the weaker sex.

THE SEMITES.

Of this division of the Caucasic stock two branches are represented in North-East Africa· 1. The Yoktanides, or Himyarites, from prehistoric times, mainly in the Abyssinian highlands beyond the Egyptian frontier—Tigré, Amhara, Bogos,[11] and others speaking more or less corrupt dialects of the Gheez or old Himyaritic language of South Arabia. 2 The Ismaelites, or Arabs proper, a few probably from prehistoric times, especially in Senaar, but the great majority since the Muhammadan invasion in the seventh century, chiefly in the steppe-lands west of the Nile from the Sobat confluence northwards to Dongola. Some of the early arrivals, such as the Jowabere (جوابرى) and El Gharbíye (العربيه), appear to have settled in the Nile Valley south of Egypt, where they became assimilated in speech to the surrounding Nubian population. Many others moved westwards through Kordofan and Dar-Fur to Wadai and the Tsad basin, and, speaking generally, no part of North and North-East Africa except the Abyssinian uplands can be said to be entirely free from the Arab element.

Unfortunately this is also the disturbing element, but for the presence of which there would be no fanaticism, no slave-dealers, no Mahdis, no "Egyptian question," to confound the councils of European statesmanship. Proud, ignorant, bigoted, and insolent, these Arab tribes "are for the most part nomads or wanderers, each within certain well-known limits All are large owners of cattle, camels, horses, and slaves. These last, along with the Arab women generally cultivate some fields of dura, or corn, sufficient for the wants of the tribe. The Arab himself would consider it a disgrace to practise any manual labour. He is essentially a hunter, a robber, and a warrior, and, after caring for his cattle, devotes all his energies to slave-hunting and war."[12]

Some of these Arab tribes are very numerous and powerful They command great influence amongst the surrounding populations, and are often in a position to defy the supreme authority, or compel it to accept their conditions in the administration of Eastern Sudán. The most important are the Sheygyeh, Robabat, Jahn, and Kababish, between Dongola and Khartum; the Baqqára,[13] thence southwards nearly to the Sobat confluence, the Homran, Rekhabin, and Alawin of Senaar; the Hamr, El-Homr, Mahámid, and Habameh, of Kordofan and Dar-Fur. In general, the Semitic type is fairly well preserved, although the Sheygyeh and some others are distinguished by a dark, almost black, complexion. Traces of intermixture with the Negroes are also evident in many districts, while complete fusion of the two elements seems to have taken place in parts of Senaar and Nubia In religion all alike are zealous Muhammadans, to whom some system of domestic slavery seems almost indispensable   Hence even were the export of slaves to Egypt and Arabia suppressed, the institution would still survive in a mitigated form in the interior of the country.

THE HAMITES

As common members of the Caucasic family, the Hamites must be regarded as remote kinsmen of the Semites.   But while the latter are comparatively recent intruders from Arabia, the former constitute the true indigenous element in North Africa. In Egyptian Sudán they are found both west and east of the Nile   In the west, however, they are represented only by the Zoghâwa, Baele, and one or two other members of the Tibu group settled chiefly in the north-western districts of Dar-Fur

The true affinities of the Tibus, long a subject of discussion among anthropologists, may now be determined in the light of the fresh materials recently brought to Europe by Dr. Nachtigal, and partly published in his monumental work, "Sahara und Sudán."[14]   The Tibu domain comprises the whole of East Sahara from about 12° E. longitude to the Egyptian frontier, and from Fezzan southwards to Kanem, Wadai, and Dar-Fur.   There are two main branches . 1. The Teda, or Northern Tibus, possibly to be identified with the Tedamansu, a tribe of Garamantes placed by Ptolemy in Tripolitana , 2 The Daza, or Southern Tibus, through whom they gradually merge southwards in the Kanembu, Kanuri, Zoghâwa, Baele, and other Negro or Negroid peoples of Central and Eastern Sudán   The Tibu language follows precisely the same course, passing from the Northern and primitive Téda through the more highly developed Daza to the mixed Kanuri and other forms in the Tsad basin

But the physical and linguistic features revolve, so to say, in different planes, implying apparent antagonism between the ethnical and philological conditions.   Both are found in their purest and most original state amongst the Northern Tedas, a point that has been clearly established by Nachtigal   But while the Teda physical type is not to be distinguished from that of the neighbouring Imoshagh or Tuarik (Berber Hamites) of the Western Sahara, the Teda language shows no affinity either with the Hamitic or the Negro groups.   It stands entirely apart, constituting ˉ the nucleus of a widespread linguistic family with extensive ramifications in Dar-Fur, Wadai, Kanem, Bornu, Baghirmi, and generally throughout Central Sudán. In this region it appears to have been profoundly affected by Negro influences ; but no such influences can be detected in the Tibesti uplands, probably the cradle of the Tibu race and the centre of dispersion of the Tibu language

It follows that the Tibus must be regarded as a branch of the Hamitic stock, who, during their long isolation in Tibesti, have had time to develop an independent idiom no longer traceable to a common Tibu-Berber source. A notable feature of this idiom is the absence of grammatical gender, placing it even on a lower level than many Negro tongues of the Upper Nile and Kilima-Njaro regions. It appears, however, to supply what may be called the "raw material," out of which gender has been elaborated in the Hamitic languages. Thus *o* seems to be characteristic of masculine, *d* or *t* of feminine terms, as in *o-miri* = man; *á-di* = woman. With this feminine dental may be compared the Berber *t*, which is both pre- and post-fixed, as in *akli* = negro; *taklit* = negress.

The word *omri* may serve in a way to connect the Tibu Hamites with the Galla, a chief branch of the Eastern Hamites, who also call themselves *Oromo*, Orma, Ormu = men. To these Eastern Hamites, who skirt the Indian Ocean and the Red Sea from the Equator to Egypt, and of whom the ancient Egyptians themselves were a branch, the vague terms Kushite and Ethiopian are frequently applied. By the intervening Abyssinian highlands they are divided into a southern and a northern group, the chief branches of the former being the Afars (Dankali), the Somali, Galla, Kaffa,[15] and outlying Wa-Huma, of the latter the Saho, Bogos, or Bilin (?), Beja, or Bishari; the old Egyptians, modern Kopts, and Fellahin, besides the Agau and some other scattered communities in Abyssinia.

The Wa-Huma, to whom the attention of ethnologists has scarcely yet been seriously directed, present some points of great anthropological interest, probably affording a solution of the difficulties connected with the constituent elements of the Bantu races in East Central Africa. Speke had already observed that the chiefs of the Bantu nations about the great lakes were always Wa-Huma, a pastoral people evidently of Galla stock, and originally immigrants from the Galla country. Since then it has been ascertained that several Wa-Huma communities live interspersed amongst the mixed Bantu nations of the lacustrine plateau, and J. M. Schuver was recently informed that the Negro inhabitants of the Afilo country were governed by a Galla aristocracy.[16]

From these and other indications it seems highly probable that in point of fact the Bantu peoples are fundamentally Negroes in diverse proportions affected by Wa-Huma or Galla, that is, Hamitic elements. The Wa-Huma, who, under the name of Wa-Tusi,[17] are found as far south as the U-Nyamezi country, are by recent observers unanimously described as a very fine race, with oval face, straight nose, small mouth, and generally speaking regular Caucasic features. Such a type is found everywhere cropping out amid the surrounding Negroid populations throughout the southern half of the continent, and the conclusion seems irresistible that it should be referred to these Wa-Huma or Hamitic Gallas, probably for ages advancing as conquerors from the north-east into the heart of the continent.

No distinct mention is made of the Wa-Huma speech. It is known, however, to differ from that of the Bantus proper; and when we hear that the late King M'tesa of U-Ganda spoke Galla as his mother-tongue, and was proud of his Galla ancestors, little doubt can remain on this point. The Wa-Huma are also distinguished by their intense love both of personal freedom and political autonomy, sentiments which are but feebly developed amongst the true Negro populations. Such is their horror of captivity and a foreign yoke, that those who have failed to maintain their independence are no longer regarded as true Wa-Huma. The very women, who have the misfortune to fall into the hands of the Arab slave-dealers, are looked upon as degraded for ever, and should they escape from bondage, are burnt alive by their own people. Traits of this sort would almost alone suffice to suspect at least a very large infusion of non-Negro blood in the Wa-Huma race. This element we may now trace with some confidence to the Hamites of North-East Africa as its true source.

The Afars, Somali, Galla, and other members of the Southern Hamitic group need not here detain us further. They lie mostly beyond the jurisdiction of the Egyptian Mudirs, and very few of their tribes have hitherto been brought within the sphere of civilising influences. Enough to state in a general way that their languages all belong to the Hamitic connection, forming outlying branches of the great linguistic family from the earliest times diffused throughout the whole of North Africa, and in this region corresponding to the Bantu in the southern half of the continent.

Of the northern group of Ethiopian Hamites by far the most important are the Beja, or Bishari, who have all the greater claim to the consideration of the ethnologist, that their ethnical status has hitherto been persistently ignored alike by British Cabinet Ministers, officials, and newspaper correspondents. They are the unfortunate people, many of whose tribes have recently come into collision with the British forces in the Suakin district, but who continue to be spoken of as "Arabs" by those statesmen who are unable to recognise more than two races in Egyptian Sudán, that is, the Negro and Arab. Thus on February 27th of the present year the Marquis of Hartington telegraphs to General Graham · "Tell them we are not at war with the *Arabs*, but must disperse force threatening Suakin." And General Graham himself sends a letter "written in Arabic" to the chiefs of the tribes about Trinkitat and Tokar, in which they are again assumed to be "Arabs" We all remember the ignominious fate of that now historical document, which was set up as a target and riddled by bullets, as some dangerous fetish, by those Hamitic followers of Muhammad Osman Dakanah, whose own language, the To-Bedawich, differs almost as much from Arabic as does that of the British troops itself All this immediately preceded the sanguinary engagement of El Teb, and it may be asserted with Sir Stafford Northcote, though for reasons different from those implied by him, that "if the position of England had been such as it ought to have been, we should have had none of the slaughter which then took place." In fact, had a moderate amount of attention been paid by our Foreign Office to the true ethnical conditions in Egyptian Sudán, most of the complications might probably have been avoided that have since arisen in that distracted region. But the necessity for a systematic study of ethnology has not yet made itself apparent to the rulers of the most multifarious complexity of tribes and peoples ever entrusted to the charge of a single Administration

The Bejas are the true autochthonous element in East Nubia, where they occupy the whole of the arid steppe-lands stretching from the Nile to the Red Sea, and from the Abyssinian frontier northwards as far as the parallel of Keneh and Kosseir in Upper Egypt.[18] Their main divisions are the Ababdeh, to be identified with Pliny's Gabadei about the Egyptian frontier, the Hadendoah, Hassanab, and Demilab, along the coastlands, and as far inland as the El-Matre wells on the Suakin-Berber route; the Bishari proper, thence westwards to the Nile; the Amarar and Ashraf north from the Suakin-Berber route, and here and there overlapping the Bishari, the Kamlab, Halenga, and Beni-Amer along the Abyssinian frontier from the Nile to the Red Sea in the order here given

By Linant Bey (Linant de Bellefonds), one of the most intelligent observers of these peoples, they are described as of European (Caucasic) type, often very handsome, of a bronze, swarthy, or light chocolate complexion, with long, crisp, but not woolly hair, generally falling in ringlets over the shoulders.[19] So also the Macrobes, of the same region, were long ago described by Herodotus (Book III) as "the tallest and finest of men," to whom Cambyses sent envoys from their kindred of Elephantine Island, but failed to reduce Nevertheless, through long contact with the surrounding African populations the present Bejas show here and there evident traces of Negro blood, conspicuous especially in the thick lips and broad nose of some of their tribes. On the other hand, the northern or Ababdeh branch have been largely assimilated even in speech to their Arab neighbours and hereditary foes, the Antúni (Ma'azeh) of Upper Egypt.[20] All are now more or less zealous Muhammadans, occupied chiefly with camel-breeding and as caravan leaders, governed by hereditary sheikhs, and, like their Hamitic kindred elsewhere, distinguished by their personal bravery and love of freedom.

Beja, the most collective national name, may be traced through the harder Arabic form *Beya*[21] of the tenth century to the *Búga* (Βουγαειται) of the Greek and Axumite (Geez) inscriptions, and thence perhaps to the *Buka* of the hieroglyphic records. These Βουγαειταί appear to be identical with the βλέμμυες (Kopt. Balnemmoui) who are already mentioned by Strabo,[22] and who from the third to the sixth century of the new era infested the southern frontiers of Egypt. Often defeated by Aurelian and Probus, they nevertheless so continued to harass these outlying provinces of the empire, that Diocletian was at last induced to withdraw the Roman garrisons from the region of the Cataracts, replacing them by the warlike Nobatæ tribes from the great oasis of Kargey in Upper Egypt.

THE NUBAS.

The just-mentioned Nobatæ of Diocletian are commonly assumed to be the modern Nubians. But, although not yet recognised in British official reports, the Nubian race and name have even a more venerable antiquity than this statement would imply. In a passage quoted in note 22 we find mention already made by Strabo of the Νοῦβαι; and in another passage the same writer, who flourished three hundred years before the time of Diocletian, describes these Nubæ as "a great nation" dwelling in Libya, that is, Africa, along the left bank of the Nile from Meroe to the bends of the river.[23] The word itself has even been identified by some writers with the land of *Nub* or *Nob*, that is, "Gold," the region about Mount Elbeh on the Red Sea coast over against Jiddah, where the Egyptians worked the precious metal from the remotest times.

But this identification must be rejected since the discovery that the cradle of the Nuba race is not to the east but to the west of the Nile,[24] in the Kordofan highlands. The final syllable *fán* of the very word Kordo-fán is explained to mean in the Nuba language *land, country*, thus answering to the Arabic *dár*, as in Dár-Fur = the land of the *Fur* people. Both the Fur and the Kordo, if these latter are identical with the

Kargo of the Jebel-Kargo, are themselves of Nuba stock and speech, and the term Nuba is still current in Kordofan both in an ethnical and a geographical sense, indicating the Jebel-Nuba uplands inhabited by the Nuba tribe. Here, therefore, is the true home of the race, some of whom appear to have migrated northwards some two thousand years ago, settling partly in the Kargey oasis (Diocletian's Nobatæ), partly in the narrow valley of the Nile about Meroe (Strabo's Nubæ)

Since those days there have always been Nubæ, Nobatæ, or Nubians in the Nile Valley, mainly in the region of the Cataracts, and we read that after their removal hither from Kargey the Nobatæ dwelt for some time peacefully with the Blemmyes (Hamitic Bejas). They even made common cause with them against the Romans; but the confederacy was crushed by Maximinus in 451. Then the Bejas withdrew to their old homes in the Arabian desert, while the Nobatæ, embracing Christianity in 545, developed a powerful Christian state in the Nile Valley. Silco, founder of this kingdom of Dongola, as it was called from its capital, bore the title of "King of the Noubads and of all the Ethiopians," that is, of the present Nubian and Beja nations. His empire lasted for 700 years, and was finally overthrown by the Arabs in the thirteenth century, since which time the Nile Nubians have been Muhammadans. They also gradually withdrew to their present limits between Egypt and Old Dongola, the rest of their territory thence to Khartum being occupied by the Sheygyeh, Robabat, Jalin, and other powerful Arab tribes

There are thus two main divisions of the Nuba race the Nubas proper of Kordofan, found also dispersedly in Dar-Fur; and the Nile Nubas, commonly called Nubians in European books of travel, but who now call themselves Barabra [25] By the latter the term Nuba has been rejected, and is even regarded as an insult when applied to them by others The old national name appears to have fallen into discredit in the Nile Valley, where it has become synonymous with "slave," owing to the vast number of slaves supplied for ages by the Nuba populations of Kordofan and Dar-Fur.[26] The Nile Nubas themselves supply no slaves to the market. Constituting settled and semi-civilised Muhammadan communities, they are treated on a footing of perfect equality in Egypt, where large numbers are engaged as free labourers, porters, "costermongers," and in various other pursuits. They are a strong, muscular people, essentially agricultural, more warlike and energetic than the Egyptians, whom they also excel in moral qualities. Their Muhammadanism is not of a fanatical type, and although the present Mahdi is a Nubian of Dongola he has found his chief support not amongst his countrymen, but amongst the more recently converted Negroes, and especially the Arab and Hamite communities of Kordofan and other parts of Eastern Sudán.

There is a marked difference between the physical appearance of the two great branches of the Nuba race. The Nubian (Barabra) type is obviously Negroid, very dark, often almost black, with tumid lips, large black dreamy eyes, dolichocephalic head (73·72 as compared with the normal Negro 73·40, and the old Egyptian 75·58), woolly or strongly frizzled hair. The scant beard is still worn under the chin, like the figures of the Negro fugitives in the battle-pieces sculptured on the walls of the Egyptian temples. But, as amongst all mixed peoples, there are considerable deviations from the normal Nubian standard, some showing affinities to the old Egyptian, as already remarked by Blumenbach, some noted for their fine oval face and regular features, others for their long or slightly crisp hair, and bronze,[27] reddish brown, or deep mahogany complexions. In general it may be said with Burkhardt that the nose is less flat, the lips less thick, the cheekbones less prominent, the colour less dark ("of a coppery tinge"), than amongst the true Negros. The Nile Nubians must therefore be regarded as essentially a mixed race, presenting every shade of transition between the original Nuba type and the various Hamitic and Semitic elements, with which they have intermingled in the Nile Valley.

The original Nuba type itself must be studied in the Kordofan highlands, where it persists in its greatest purity. The Kordofan Nuba are unanimously described by Russeger, Petherick, Lepsius, and other intelligent observers, as emphatically a Negro race. "Negerstämme," "Negerfolk," "Negroes," "Niggers," are the unqualified terms applied to them in all books of travel, so that there can be no doubt at all on this point.[28] Its importance is obvious, for it settles the question of the true affinities of the Nile Nubians, about which so much controversy has prevailed.

It is remarkable, however, that Lepsius traces the Nile Nubians, not to the Kordofan Nubas, but directly to the Uaua Negroes of the Nile Valley. These Uaua are the oldest people, of whom there is any record, in this region. Their name occurs on a tomb at Memphis dating from the time of Pepi, sixth dynasty, 2500 B.C. They are again mentioned in the Wadi-Halfa inscription amongst the tribes reduced by Usertesen II, of the twelfth dynasty. Allusion is also made to the *Uauat* country, and in many subsequent inscriptions the Uaua figure largely as at the head of all the Negro races beyond the Egyptian frontier. In fact, the word became the conventional or stereotyped name of the Nile Negroes generally down to the time of the Ptolemies, after which it suddenly disappears from historic records.

This disappearance has not been explained. But it was probably due to the already mentioned irruption of the Bugaitæ (Bejas), by whom the Uaua were reduced, if not exterminated. There is consequently no necessary connection between them and the Nubians, whose more recent migration from Kordofan to the Nile Valley may be regarded as clearly established.

Whatever doubt might remain on this point is removed by a consideration of the linguistic argument. In his masterly treatise on the Nubian language quoted further back, Lepsius himself has shown that the speech of both branches of the Nuba race is identical, presenting merely some slight dialectic varieties, easily explained by the length of time that has elapsed since the migration. The structure is the same, and the subjoined list of a few common words in the Dongolawi of the Nile and in four Kordofan dialects shows that the vocabulary also is essentially one :—

English.	Dongolawi (Nile).	Jebel Kargo.	Jebel Kolaji.	Jebel Nuba.	Jebel Kulfán.
Mouth....	agil	ogl	aul	aljo	awol
Foot......	gedem	kogodi	kuddo	koördo	ket
Cow......	ti	ti	eh	ti	teh
Fire......	ig	ik	eka	?	ika
One......	weri	ber	bera	ber	ber
Two......	owi	orre	ora	ora	ora
Three	toski	toje	toje	toju	toju

It is incredible that the speech of the Uaua Negroes and Kordofan Nubas, if originally the same, could have maintained its identity with such slight changes as these for a period of nearly 4,400 years—that is, from the time of Pepi (2500 B.C.), when mention first occurs of the Uaua. It seems safe to conclude that, while the identity of the Nile and Kordofan Nubas is established, neither branch has any obvious or necessary connection with the extinct Uaua of the Egyptian records.

Independently of this consideration the Nubian language, first clearly elucidated by Lepsius, presents some points of interest both to the philologist and ethnologist. Its Negro character is shown in its phonology, in the complete lack of grammatical gender, and in some structural peculiarities. Such is the infix *j* inserted between the verbal root and the plural pronominal object, as in *ai tokki-j-ir* = I shake them. As in Bantu, the verbal conjugation is highly developed, presenting such a multiplicity of forms that in Lepsius' Grammar the complete paradigm of a single verb fills as many as 110 pages The Nubian language never appears to have been cultivated, or even committed to writing.[29]   Hence it is not likely to afford the key, as some have suggested, to the numerous undeciphered inscriptions occurring along the banks of the Nile as far south as Senaar.

It enables us, however, to dispose of the so-called "Nuba-Fulah" family, originally constituted of heterogeneous elements by Frederick Muller, and generally accepted by anthropologists on the authority of that distinguished ethnologist   We have already seen at the outset that the Fulahs are a non-Negro race, most probably allied to the western Hamites of the Sahara. The Fulah speech, also, appears from Krause's Grammar to be a non-Negro language, betraying not the remotest resemblance to the Nuba   Thus the Nubas are of Negro stock and speech, and so the "Nuba-Fulah" family is dissolved, its *disjecta membra* finding each its place amongst its own kindred.

Yet another point   In the light of these new revelations how fares it with Lepsius' theory, which reduces the indigenous elements in Africa to two racial and linguistic stocks, the Hamitic in the north and the Negro in the south, Sudán thus becoming an intermediate zone of transition and intermingling between these two types?   On the face of it the theory seems, so to say, too simple and symmetrical to hold good   Nature loves law and order, but in the biological world seems averse from such mathematical regularity   Nor is it found in the Dark Continent, where, besides the Hamite and Negro, account must be taken of the Hottentot, Bushman, Pigmy (Akka, Obongo, &c.), and possibly other not yet discovered autochthonous elements.

But it is on its linguistic side that the scheme of Lepsius fails most signally.   In Egyptian Sudán alone we find at least a dozen languages which can neither be traced to a common source nor in any way affiliated to Lepsius' typical orders of speech, the Hamitic and the Bantu.   Such are the Tibu (Zoghawah and Baele dialects) the Fulah of Dar-Fur, the Nuba, Basé, Dinka, Bari, Shilluk, Zandeh, Nuer, and others in the Zeriba region of the Upper Nile and in the Sobat valley   Anthropology recognises only a very limited number of physical types in the whole world, and even these are for the monogenist mere varieties of a single species   But philology recognises, not a limited, but almost an unlimited number of linguistic types, true types often differing generically and not merely specifically, and utterly incapable of being reduced even to one order of speech.[30]   Hence in other regions of the globe we everywhere find a very large number of stock languages, seventy for instance in North America, distributed amongst just two or three stock races. It would be to the last degree surprising and phenomenal, were Africa alone to form an exception to the general rule, that there is no necessary correspondence between ethnical and linguistic groups.

Subjoined are tabulated schemes of all the Eastern Sudanese and contiguous ethnical groups, with their chief subdivisions and geographical position.

I. BANTU GROUP.

Wa-Ganda.. North-west side Victoria Nyanza, from the Somerset to the Alexandria Nile (Tanguré), the most numerous and powerful Bantu nation in the region of the Great Lakes.

Wa-Nyoro .. Between Somerset Nile and Albert Nyanza.

Wa-Soga .. East from the Somerset Nile.

Wa-Gamba East of the Wa-Soga territory; limits undefined.

Wa-Karagwé West side Victoria Nyanza, from the Alexandria Nile southwards to the Wa-Zinza territory.

Wa-Songora West side of Victoria Nyanza between the Wa-Karagwé and the coast.

II. NEGRO GROUP.

Kavirondo .. ⎫
Kuri .. ⎬ East side Victoria Nyanza, dominent from the Wa-Soga territory to the Kerewé Island, south-east corner of the lake. Speech appears to be Negro, and akin to Shilluk.
Kara .. ⎭

Nanda .. Nanda uplands north of Kavirondo, fierce wild tribes of uncertain affinities.

Masai .. Kilimanjaro, thence westwards towards Victoria Nyanza; national name Oigob; speech distinctly Negro, akin to the Bari.

Kwafi .. West of Mount Kenia, north of the Masai territory; classed by Krapf with the Hamitic group, but type seems Negro.

Shefalu .. North U-Nyoro, akin to the Shilluks.

Madi ⎫
Shuli ⎬ Between the Lower Somerset Nile and the Madi mountains, and limited westwards by the Bahr-el-Jebel.
Laboré ⎭

Janghey ⎫
Fallanj ⎬ Lower Sobat basin.
Niuak ⎭

Bari .. Both sides Bahr-el-Jebel, 4°—5° N., limited northwards by the Shir territory.

Monbuttu .. About headwaters of the river Welle, beyond the Egyptian frontier.

Zandeh .. From south-west frontier Egyptian Sudán for unknown distance westwards; are the Niam-Niam of the Nilotic tribes.

Mittu ⎧ A-Madi ⎫ Moro district north of Monbuttuland. The Mittu
(*Mattu*) .. ⎨ Madi-Kaya ⎬ call their country Moro, which is not an ethnical
⎩ Abbakah ⎪ but a geographical name (Schweinfurth, "Heart
   Luba ⎭ of Africa," I, p. 403.

Bongo (Dor) Upper course Tondy and Jur rivers, thence to Zandeh frontier.

Shir.. .. Bahr-el-Jebel 5°—6° N., between the Dinka and Bari territories.

Rol ..   .. ⎫
Agar   ..   Tribes of uncertain affinity along Rol river, east of the Bongo
Soft..   ..   and Mittu.
Lehsi   .. ⎭

Nuer   .. { Byor / Ror } Along lower course Bahr-el-Jebel, 7°—9° N.

Dinka   .. { Abuyo, Agar, Ajak, Aliab, Arol, Atwot, Awan, Bor, Donjol, Jur, Gok, Rish } Along Bahr-el-Jebel, and right bank White Nile, 6°—12° N. Largest of all the Nilotic Negro tribes (Beltrami).

Shilluk   .. { Kwati, Dyakin, Dyok, Roah } Left bank Bahr-el-Jebel and White Nile, 9°—12° N

Dwuir   .. ⎫
Ayarr   ..
Mok .   ·   Unclassed tribes south of the Dinkas, north east of the Bongos,
Tondy   ..   7°—8° N., between Molmul and Ruah rivers ; probably akin
Bót .   ..   to the Bongos.
Ayell   .. ⎭

Takruri   ..   Gallibat district, Abyssinian frontier, originally from Dar-Fur (James's " Wild Tribes of the Sudán, ' p. 30).

Funj   ..   The dominant race in Senaar, supposed to be of Shilluk stock, but now largely mixed with the Arabs of that region

Krej   .. ⎫ About headwaters of the Bahr-el-Arab, beyond Egyptian
Fertit   .. ⎭ frontier

III. NUBA GROUP.

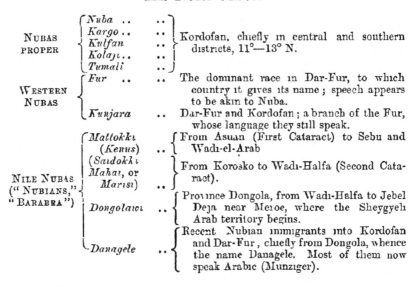

NUBAS PROPER { Nuba ..   .. / Kargo..   .. / Kulfan   .. / Kolaji..   .. / Tumali   .. } Kordofan, chiefly in central and southern districts, 11°—13° N.

WESTERN NUBAS { Fur   ..   .. } The dominant race in Dar-Fur, to which country it gives its name ; speech appears to be akin to Nuba.

           Kunjara   ..   Dar-Fur and Kordofan ; a branch of the Fur, whose language they still speak.

NILE NUBAS (" NUBIANS," " BARABRA") {

Mattokki (Kenus)   ..   { From Asuan (First Cataract) to Sebu and Wadi-el-Arab

(Saidokhi Mahai, or Marisi)   ..   { From Korosko to Wadi-Halfa (Second Cataract).

Dongolawi   ..   { Province Dongola, from Wadi-Halfa to Jebel Deja near Meroe, where the Sheygyeh Arab territory begins.

Danagele   ..   { Recent Nubian immigrants into Kordofan and Dar-Fur, chiefly from Dongola, whence the name Danagele. Most of them now speak Arabic (Munziger).
}

IV. SEMITIC GROUP.

(a) HIMYARITIC OR ABYSSINIAN BRANCH[31]

{ Dahalaki   ..   Great Dahalak Island near Massawa
Massuai   ..   The mixed population of Massawa, of Tigré speech.

Hotumlu   .. ⎫
Karneshim   ..   Mudun (Samhar) coast district about Massawa and as far as Aqiq.
Az-Shuma
Dokono ⎭ }

(a) **HIMYARITIC OR ABYSSINIAN BRANCH**[31] **(continued)**	*Habab* .. .. *Bejuk* .. .. *Mensa* .. *Bogos (Bilin)*[32] *Talue* . .. *Marea*	Anseba province, north-east frontier of Abyssinia inland from Mndun.
	Algeden .. *Sabderat* .. *Dembela* ..	Beit-Bidel and Dembela districts, about the head streams of the Barka (Baraka) and Mareb (Gash) rivers, west of Anseba
	Harrar ..	Abyssinian enclave in Somaliland, east from Shoa, 9° 40′ N., 42° E.
	Tigré	The predominant nation in North Abyssinia
	Amhara ..	The predominant nation in South Abyssinia, now politically subject to the Tigré
(b) **ISMAELITIC OR ARAB BRANCH**	*Sheygyeh (Shaikieh)* ..	From Dongola along left bank Nile to Abu-Hammed Noted for their extremely dark complexion, yet claiming to be of unmixed Arab descent.
	Robabat ..	From Abu-Hammed to the Atbara confluence
	Hassanieh ..	About the Atbara confluence, between the Robabat and Jalin north and south
	Homran ..	Middle course of the Atbara and Mareb rivers as far as the Basé (Kunama) territory.
	Shukrieh .. *Dobeina* .. *Yemanieh* ..	Lower and Middle Atbara (left bank), and southwards to Senaar.
	Jalin (Jahalin)	Mainly about the Blue Nile confluence, Khartum district; but widely diffused as traders and settlers throughout Senaar, Taka, Kordofan, Dar-Fur, and even Kaffa[33]
	Kababish[34] ..	Widely spread west of the Nile beween 12°—15° N., but especially along the route from Obeid (Kordofan) to the Nile at Dongola. The name means "Goatherds," although they are also large breeders of horses and camels.
	Baqqára[34] ..	Mainly south of the Kababish along west bank of the Nile and Bahr-el-Arab nearly to its source The term means "cowherds" (see note 13)

V. HAMITIC GROUP.

TIBU BRANCH	*Baele* .. .. *Ennedi* .. *Zogháwa* ..	North Dar-Fur; thence north-westwards to Wanganja and Borku; speech akin to the Dasa or Southern Tibu; type Negroid.
BERBER BRANCH	*Fulah*	West Dar-Fur, where a few Fulah communities have penetrated in recent times from the Tsad basin.
SOUTH ETHIOPIAN BRANCH	**OROMO OR GALLA.**	
	Ittu	Ittu Mountains, 41°—42° E, 9°—10° N.
	Carayu ..	South-east of Ankober.
	Dawari ..	West from Tajuria Bay.
	Wolo . ..	West of Lake Ardibbo
	Worro-Babbo ..	East of Lakes Ardibbo and Haic

SOUTH ETHIOPIAN BRANCH (continued)	OROMO OR GALLA (continued)	Mecha ..	South of Gojam.
		Raya ..	West of Zebul
		Asabo ..	
		Lango ..	Somerset Nile between Foweira and Magungo.
		Wa-Huma ..	Intermingled with the Bantu populations of the eastern equatorial regions
		Wa-Tusi..	
		Sidama ..	Kaffaland, south-west of Shoa, hitherto wrongly grouped with the Nubas.[35]
	SOMALI	Isa .	Between Zeilah, Harrar, and Berbera
		Isa-Ishaai-Modoba ..	
		Gudabirsi ..	
		Habr-Awal ..	
		Habr-Gerhajis ..	Uplands south of Berbera
		Gadohursi ..	East of Berbera to the Indian Ocean
		Dalbahantu ..	
		Warsingali ..	
		Mijjerthain ..	
CENTRAL ETHIOPIAN BRANCH	AFAR (ADAL OR DANAKIL)	Debnet ..	Coastlands between Abyssinia and the Red Sea, from Zula Bay to Strait of Bab-el-Mandeb.[36]
		Asoba .	
		Assa-Imara ..	
		Sidi-Habura ..	
		Galeila ..	
	Khamir ..	Lasta district ..	Abyssinia.
	Agau ..	Quara district ..	
	Agaumeder ..	Gondar district ..	
	Khamant ..		
	Saho, or Shoho	North-east frontier, Abyssinia	
NORTH ETHIOPIAN BRANCH (BEJA DIVISION)	Hadendoa ..	Between Suakin and the Nile, thence southwards to the Abyssinian frontier	
	Bishari ..		
	Beni-Amer ..	Along north frontier, Abyssinia, both largely affected by Semitic elements, and often wrongly classed with the Abyssinian Himyarites[37]	
	Halenga ..		
	Amarar ..	Along the coast from Suakin northwards to Ras-Benass and thence inland.	
	Ababdeh	Upper Egypt and Arabian Desert, from Koseir southwards to the neighbourhood of Wadi-Halfa, partly assimilated to the Arab tribes on their northern frontier.	

VI. UNCLASSIFIED GROUPS.

Barea Basé or Kunáma	About middle course Mareb and headwaters of the Barka, north frontier Abyssinia; closely related in habits, type, &c., but of different speech (Nere-bena and Bazena-awia), apparently the true aborigines of Abyssinia[38]
Birkit .. Masalit .. Abu-Sarib .. Tala Bikka ..	Dar-Fur, chiefly towards Wadai frontier, of doubtful affinities (Barth, III, p 539)
Assiri ..	The aborigines of Kordofan, apparently extinct or absorbed in the Fogelé and Nubas

Tegelé	..	Large nation south Kordofan, usually classed as Nubas, but
Tekelé	.	quite distinct.[39]
Qadeyat	..	In thirty villages, south and east of Mount Kordofan; said to be of Funj origin
Musabat	..	Obeid district, Kordofan, claim descent from the Kunjara of
Museıbat	..	Dar-Fur, where some are still found, all now speak Arabic exclusively.

NOTES

[1] "Nubische Grammatik," Einleitung.

[2] "Im Gegentheil drangen uns diese Thatsachen zu dem Schlusse hin, dass auf der eine Seite die fulische Sprache in ihrer ersten Anlage, sowie die hamito-semitischen Sprachen, und dann auf der andern das fulische Volk, sowie Hamito-Semiten eines und desselben Ursprungs seien. Aus diesem Grunde nennen wir die Fulen die Ur- oder Proto-Hamiten."—*Ein Beitrag zur Kenntniss der Fulischen Sprache* (Leipzig, 1884, p 11).

[3] Thus Lieut.-Colonel Stewart, in his otherwise valuable "Report on the Sudán for 1883". "Besides the main division of the people into Arab and Negro, they are again subdivided into a number of tribes and sub-tribes, some sedentery, and others nomad" (p 8)   These sub-tribes are not further specified but in what follows all are treated either as Arabs or Negroes

[4] 'Nature," April 17, 1884, p 581

[5] "Grammatica e Vocabolario della lingua Denka," Rome, 1880, p. 231.

[6] In Senaar alone the Arabs reckon as many as six gradations between the pure Negro and the Semite 1. El-Asraf, or yellow, 2 El-Kat Fatalobin, the Abyssinian, 3 El-Akdar, or red, 4. El-Azraq, or blue; 5 El-Ahsdar, or "green", 6 Ahbit, the Nubian.

[7] Schweinfurth, "Heart of Africa"

[8] Rev T Wakefield, in "Proceedings of the Geographical Society, for December, 1882

[9] Lepsius, *op cit*, "Einleitung."

[10] Schweinfurth, *op cit*, ii, p. 93.

[11] The position of the Bogos or Bilín, who occupy a debatable tract at the north-east corner of Abyssinia on the Egyptian frontier, is somewhat doubtful Leo Reinisch regards their speech as a Gheez dialect ("Die Bilín Sprache," Vienna, 1882), yet he classes them subsequently with the neighbouring Hamite peoples, as will be seen further on

[12] Lieut.-Colonel Stewart's "Report on the Sudán for 1883," p 8

[13] The term *Baqqára*, unknown in the Arab national genealogies, has given rise to some misunderstanding It is not the name of any particular tribe, but an expression applied collectively to all tribes which breed and deal in cattle, in contradistinction to those whose wealth consists in horses and camels Hence there are Baqqára in many parts of Sudán, although they are chiefly concentrated about the left bank of the White Nile, and further west towards the head-streams of the Bahr-el-Arab (Baqqára-el-Homi). The word is derived from بقر = *baqar* = an ox

[14] Two volumes only have so far appeared (Berlin, 1879, 1881). The remainder, with rich philological data, are anxiously awaited by students of African ethnology

[15] At Keren in the Bogos country Leo Reinisch tells us that in 1880 he picked up enough of the Kaffa language from three slaves to determine its connection with the Hamitic family. To the same connection he refers the Agaumeder and Khamant of Gondar, and some others on the north frontier of Abyssinia, about whose true affinities some doubt still prevails ("Oester-reichische Monatschr f den Orient," March 15, 1884, p 94)

[16] "Afilo wurde mir vom Lega-König als ein Negerland bezeichnet, welches von einer Galla-Aristokratie beherrscht wird" (Petermann's Mittheilungen, 1883, v, p. 194)

[17] And are no doubt also known by other names. Thus the Wa-Taturu shepherds of U-Kerewé Island in Lake Victoria Nyanza appear to belong to the same connection They are described by Stanley as " light-coloured, straight, thin-nosed, and thin-lipped," in contrast to their Wa-Kerewé neighbours, "a mixture of the Ethiopic and Negro type." ("Through the Dark Continent," vol i, p 251.)

[18] That this region was occupied by the Beja from remote times appears evident from Macrizi, whose account of this people in his "History of Egypt" (end of fourteenth century) is drawn from the Isthakhri (tenth century) and other older records "Le pays qu' habite ce peuple commence au bourg nommé Kharbah, près duquel est la mine d'émeraudes Le pays des Bedjas se termine aux premières frontières de l'Abyssinie. Ce peuple habite l'intérieur de la presqu'île d'Egypte jusqu'aux bords de la mer, du côté qui regarde les îles de Souaken, de Baza (Massáwah), et de Dahlak" (Quatremère's translation, in "Mémoires sur l'Egypte," 1811, ii, p 135.)

[19] "L'Etbaye, pays habité par les Bicharieh" (Paris, 1868)

[20] These Ababdeh are very widespread, stretching from Keneh southwards to the Second Cataract at Wadi-Halfa, where they meet the Kensi Nubians on the west, and the Bishari on the east. Their chief tribes, some of which also appear to speak Nubian, are the Nemráb, Gawaheh, Shawáhir (Khawáhil), Abudein, Meleikab, Tokára, and Oshabáb Russeger ("Reise," ii, Part 3, p. 193) estimates their number at about 40,000, nearly equally distributed between Egypt and Nubia

[21] The Arabic $\overline{}$, now generally pronounced j, was originally hard, like the Hebrew $\mathfrak{z}$, as we see in the geographical term *Nejd*, by the local tribes still pronounced *Negd* Hence *Bega* = *Beja*

[22] Λοιπὰ δὲ τὰ πρὸς νότον, Τρωγλοδύται, βλέμμυες, καὶ Νοῦβαι καὶ Μεγάβαροι οἱ ὑπὲρ Συήνης Αἰθίοπες (Book 17, § 53.)

[23] Ἐ'ξ ἀριστερῶν δὲ ῥύσεως τοῦ Νείλου Νοῦβαι κατοικοῦσιν εν τῇ Λιβύῃ, μέγα ἔθνος, &c (Book 17, p. 1117, Oxford ed, 1807.)

[24] This is also confirmed by Ptolemy, who (iv, 8) speaks of the Nubæ as "maxime occidentales Avalitarum"

[25] Plural of Berberi, that is, people of Berber, although at present they do not reach so far up the Nile as that town But during the eighteenth century this place acquired considerable influence as capital of a large Nubian state tributary to the Funj Kings of Senaar It is still an important station on the Nile just below the Atbara confluence at the point where the river approaches nearest to the Red Sea coast at Suakin. It may here be mentioned that the term *Barabra* is referred by some authorities, not to the town of Berber, but to the *Barabara* people, whose name occurs amongst the 113 tribes recorded in the inscription on a gateway of Thutmes, by whom they were reduced about 1700 B C This identification seems to some extent confirmed by the generic name *Kens* applied in the same inscription to many of these "Ethiopian tribes," and still surviving in the form of Kenus (plural of Kensi), the name of the northern division of the Nubian (Barabra) people towards the Egyptian frontier. It is further strengthened by a later inscription of Ramses II in Karnak (1400 B C), where mention again occurs of the *Beraberata*, one of the southern races conquered by him Hence Brugsch ("Reisebericht aus Ægypten," pp 127 and 155) is inclined to regard the modern "Barabra" as a true ethnical name confused in classic times with the Greek and Roman *Barbarus*, but which has resumed its historic value since the Moslem conquest

[26] Thus in Sakakini's tabular returns of the average prices of slaves sold in Egypt from 1870 to 1880, all, of whatever *provenance*, are grouped under two heads—"Nubians" and "Abyssinians," none being true Nubians or Abyssinians, but either Nubas and other Negroes from Kordofan and the Upper Nile, or else Barea, Basé, Shan-Gallas, and other Negroid peoples from the Abyssinian

uplands. According to these returns the latter command the highest prices in the slave market, £20 to £50 for adults, the Nubas fetching only from £18 to £40

[27] The bronze shade is also noticed by Lepsius, *op. cit.*, p. 71. "Bei den Nubiern herrscht eine dunkle Broncefarbe vor, dunkler als die der Habessinier." He adds · "Der alte Negertypus bricht nicht selten wieder ziemlich deutlich durch, namentlich ist das Wollhaar ziemlich häufig"

[28] All have woolly hair, says Ruppel ("Reisen in Nubien"), pouting thick lips, short flat nose, complexion quite black. Further comment is needless.

[29] It is noteworthy, however, that Eutychius of Alexandria (930) includes the "Nubi" among the six kinds of writing. which he tells us in a somewhat doubtful passage were current amongst the Hamitic peoples.

[30] For an explanation of this apparent antagonism the reader is referred to the monograph, "On the Ethnology and Philology of the Asiatic Races," appended to the volume on Asia, by A. H. Keane, in the Stanford Series, 1882, pp 691, *et seq*

[31] The "Ethiopian" of some, the "Agazi" of other writers, the latter term denoting peoples of Geez speech "Alle diese Völker haben einen innern Zusammenhang, sie sind Abyssinier, alte Christen, und bedienen sich des reinsten athiopischen Idioms, des Tigré" (Munziger, *op. cit.*, p. 73). This use of the term "Ethiopian" is very confusing, as it is also, and more properly, employed as the collective name of the eastern division of the Hamitic family. The Himyarites (Abyssinians) are intruders from Arabia, the Hamites are the true autochthones, hence best entitled to the title of "Ethiopian," which by the ancients was applied, although somewhat vaguely, to all the native populations stretching south from the frontier of Egypt proper.

[32] The Bogos are classed by Reinisch (*loc. cit*, p. 94) with the Hamites, or "Kushites," as he calls them But he elsewhere rightly affiliates them to the Abyssinian Semites, as speaking a pure Tigié (Geez) dialect, herein agreeing with Munziger in his "Ostafrikanische Studien," who is our best authority on these fragmentary ethnical groups on the north and north-east frontiers of Abyssinia

[33] The Jalin claim special consideration as the most numerous, intelligent, and purest of all the Sudanese Arabs They trace their descent from Abbas, uncle of the Prophet, but their Arabic speech, preserved and spoken with great purity, indicates the Hejas as their original home The chief Jalin tribes, as enumerated by Munziger, are. Muhammadab, Mikringa, Bagelab, Uádieh, Gebâlab, Kahab, Gummieh, Gummeab, Geieshab Nifeab, Sadab, Jaudallahab, Mekaberab, Meirefab, Mosellemab, Omarab, Timerab, Kitejab, Giaberab, Ahab, Ginberab, Seidab, Shatinab, Megiadab. The final *ab* of these tribal names is not an Arabic, but a Beja patronymic ending, borrowed from the neighbouring Hadendoahs of the Mareb Valley, with whom they have long been intimately associated. Some of the Jalin tribes of the Baika district have even adopted the To-Bedawieh language, and pass for Hamites.

[34] "Es ist nicht unmöglich dass die beiden Völker [Kababish and Baqqára] von einem Stamme entsprossen, sich die Weide vertheilt haben, wodurch die Trennung stereotyp wurde Die Kuhhirten hielten sich an den grasigen Suden, die Kababish an den trockenen aber von Mimosen stark bewaldeten Norden, der allein dem Kameel und der Ziege Convenirt." (Munziger, *op. cit*, p. 561)

[35] The natives of Kaffa, whose affinity to the Gallas has now been determined by Leo Reinisch, are collectively called Sidama by G Chiarini in "Memorie della Società Geografica Italiana," I, Part 2, 1878

[36] Afar appears to be the most general national name, Adal that of the dominant tribe, Danakil (plural Dankali and Danakli) is the name by which they are known to their Arab and Hamite neighbours. Chiarini (*loc cit*) recognises the close relationship of Somah and Galla, but asserts that the Afar language "ha ben poco di commune colla galla"

[37] The Halenga of the Mareb river are, however, said to be of undoubted Amharic descent.

[38] "Sie sind wohl der Ueberrest des alten Abyssinischen Reiches vor der

Einwanderung der Semiten" (Munziger, *op cit*, p 76). The type of the Basé (whose true name is Kunáma), as described and figured by F L James ("Wild Tribes of the Sudán" (London, 1883), seems distinctly Negroid In the Preface, p. 1, of that work, they are stated to be "of a totally different type, much blacker and more closely allied to the pure Negro than any of their neighbours." Yet Munziger asserts that the "sogennante Negertypus fehlt" (p 467). The point must be finally decided by a study of their language, of which nothing appears to be known. Of the Barca there are two divisions, those of the Hagr district who call themselves Nere, and those of Mogareb There is no general national name, *Barea*, meaning "slave," being simply an abusive term applied to them by the Abyssinians

[39] "Die Sprache von Tegelé hat mit dem Nuba nichts gemein; ein genaueres Studium der erstern hat mich Russegei's Classification entgegen, davon überzeugt" (Munziger, ' Ostafrikanische Studien," p 551) The same writer, a personal observer, assures us (p. 557) that there is absolutely nothing of the conventional Negro type about them, and as their language is neither Arabic, Hamitic, nor Nuba, their true position remains still to be determined.

Harrison and Sons, Printers in Ordinary to Her Majesty, St Martin's Lane

CPSIA information can be obtained at www.ICGtesting.com
Printed in the USA
BVOW09s1038060415

394876BV00016B/211/P